A Guide to the Life of Horace Walpole (1717–1797),
Fourth Earl of Orford, as Illustrated by an Exhibition
Based on the Yale Edition of His Correspondence

Wilmarth S. Lewis by Gardner Cox, 1970, holding Walpole's Notebook, 1786 (in the Beinecke Library)

A Guide to the Life of Horace Walpole (1717–1797),

Fourth Earl of Orford, as Illustrated by an Exhibition

Based on the Yale Edition of His Correspondence

W. S. Lewis

The Beinecke Rare Book and Manuscript Library

October–December 1973

Published for the Yale University Library

by Yale University Press, New Haven and London, 1973

Designed by John O. C. McCrillis
and set in Baskerville type.
Printed in the United States of America by
The Meriden Gravure Company, Meriden, Connecticut.

Published in Great Britain, Europe, and Africa by
Yale University Press, Ltd., London.
Distributed in Latin America by Kaiman & Polon,
Inc., New York City; in Australasia and Southeast
Asia by John Wiley & Sons Australasia Pty. Ltd.,
Sydney; in India by UBS Publishers' Distributors Pvt.,
Ltd., Delhi; in Japan by John Weatherhill, Inc., Tokyo.

Preface

This exhibition commemorates the start of the Yale Edition of Horace Walpole's Correspondence forty years ago. To celebrate it our thirty-six published volumes are shown with the proof or typescript of the remaining six or seven volumes, but the final index of several hundred thousand entries, to be published in 1978 in six volumes, we are leaving to the imagination. That terminal date is nearly thirty years later than the one I had in mind in 1933, a delay caused by the more than two thousand letters that have turned up since then and the time needed, which I misjudged badly, for four or five editors and their assistants to provide full annotation of the text.

The exhibition is arranged in the order the volumes have appeared. Each volume is open to a passage that mentions an object—a book, manuscript, picture, or whatever. With it is the object mentioned or one closely affiliated with it. An example of the object itself is the copy of *The Castle of Otranto* that Walpole sent William Cole (No. 2); an example of a closely affiliated object is the manuscript of Louis XVI's translation of Walpole's *Historic Doubts of Richard III* (No. 5). The objects range chronologically in Walpole's life from the copy of Watteau he made in his twentieth year to the last codicil to his will written shortly before he died sixty years later. All are from the Lewis Walpole Library at Farmington, Connecticut. They illustrate Walpole's interests and accomplishments, which he recorded not only for his correspondents, but for us, posterity, whom he addressed as his 'masters.'

Also shown are the ancillary works compiled by Professor Allen T. Hazen: *A Bibliography of the Strawberry Hill Press,* 1942, and his additions and corrections to it recently issued by Messrs Dawsons of Pall Mall in their reprint of the original edition; *A Bibliography of Horace Walpole,* 1948; and *A Catalogue of Horace Walpole's Library,* 3 vols, 1969. Walpole's books referred to are identified by the cue-title 'Hazen' followed by the number of the book in the *Catalogue.*

In planning and carrying out this guide to Walpole's life, my first thanks are due to a member of the Walpole Advisory Committee, the Director of the Beinecke Library, Professor Louis L. Martz, and his staff who gave infinite time and thought to setting up the exhibition. For helping me choose the objects shown I am indebted to my colleague of the Yale Walpole for thirty-nine years, Warren Hunting Smith, to Allen T. Hazen, now retired from Columbia, who has been a coadjutor for thirty-five years, and to his colleagues of the Walpole Advisory Committee, Bernhard Knollenberg, sometime Librarian of Yale, and Professor George B. Cooper of Trinity College, Hartford. I also wish to thank Mrs. Louis L. Martz, who has been an editor of the Yale Walpole for over thirty years, and her younger associates in it, Lars Troide and John Riely.

Following the practice of the Yale Walpole, the text of the letters has been normalized, but Walpole's punctuation and spelling of proper names have been retained.

W.S.L.

October 1973

Illustrations

Frontispiece: Wilmarth S. Lewis by Gardner Cox, 1970, holding Walpole's
        Notebook, 1786

1. Walpole's Notebook, 1786
2. Walpole's Copy of *The Castle of Otranto,* 1765, Presented to William Cole
3. Paul Sandby's View of the East and South Fronts of Strawberry Hill, ca 1783
4. Mme du Deffand's Letter in the Name of Mme de Sévigné
5. Louis XVI's Translation of Walpole's *Historic Doubts of Richard III*
6. Walpole's Copy of the Strawberry Hill *Grammont,* 1772
7. Walpole to Mme du Deffand, 13 January 1775
8. Snuff-Box with Tonton's Portrait
9. Walpole's 'Portrait' of Mme du Deffand, 1766
10. Newstead Abbey by J. C. Barrow, 1793
11. Walpole's Copy of *Stowe: A Description,* 1768
12. Little Strawberry Hill or Cliveden by Mary Berry
13. The Garden at Little Strawberry Hill (Cliveden) by J. C. Barrow, 1791
14. The First Page of Walpole's 'Short Notes' of His Life
15. A Copy of Watteau, by Walpole, 1737
16. Gray's and Bentley's Drawings of Stoke House for Gray's 'Long Story'
17. Grignion's Engraving of Bentley's Drawing
18. George Dance's Drawing of Walpole, 1793
19. Walpole Charged with Chatterton's Death
20. Walpole's Title-Page to the Mann Correspondence
21. Walpole's 'Persian' Letter to Lord Lincoln
22. Sir Robert Walpole's Last Words
23. Serendipity
24. The Book of Venetian Arms
25. The First Copy of Gray's *Odes,* 1757
26. Sir Robert Walpole's Birth-Date
27. One of the 'Tracts of George the Third'
28. 'View of Richmond-hill, Twickenham,' by Pars, 1772

29. Walpole's Pocket Notebook, 1780–1783
30. Conversation Piece by Thomas Patch of Lord Beauchamp and His Friends, 1765
31. Sir Horace Mann by John Astley, 1752
32. Lady Diana Beauclerk's Drawings for Walpole's *Mysterious Mother*, 1776
33. Walpole on Garrick's Alteration of *Hamlet*
34. The Draft of Walpole's Last Codicil to His Will
35. Allan Ramsay's Portrait of Walpole, 1758
36. Walpole's First Volume of Bunbury's Prints
37. The Duchess of Portland's Sale, 1786
38. General Fitzwilliam's Tribute to Walpole
39. Bentley's Designs for the Library at Strawberry Hill
40. Chute's Designs for the Library at Strawberry Hill
41. Sir Robert Walpole by Sir Edward Walpole
42. Walpole's Sketches of Strawberry Hill Before and After Its Alteration
43. Miss Berry as Editor
44. *Poetical Amusements at a Villa Near Bath*, 1775
45. Grosvenor Bedford's Copy of Walpole's *Aedes Walpolianae*, 1747
46. Col. Charles and Lady Mary Churchill and Their Eldest Son by Eccardt, ca 1750
47. The Duc de Nivernais's Translation of Walpole's *Modern Gardening*, 1785
48. One of Bertie Greatheed's Drawings in Walpole's Copy of the Bodoni *Castle of Otranto*, 1791
49. The Manuscript of the Journal of the Printing Office
50. *Prints Engraved by Various Persons of Quality*
51. Walpole's Last *Memoirs*, 1783–1791
52. Bentley's Frontispiece to Walpole's *Last Ten Years of George II*
53. Walpole's Copy of Sandford's *Kings of England*, 1677
54. Mason's Alterations to Walpole's *Mysterious Mother*
55. Walpole's Postscript to His *Historic Doubts of Richard III*, 1793

A Summary of Horace Walpole's Life

Born in London, September 24, 1717 OS, the third surviving son of Sir Robert Walpole, the Prime Minister, and Catherine Shorter Walpole.

He was at Eton from 1727 to 1734 and at King's College, Cambridge, from 1735 to 1738, leaving without taking a degree.

His mother died in 1737.

In 1739, he set out on a two-and-a-half year Grand Tour to France and Italy, taking the poet Thomas Gray as his companion.

While abroad his father had him elected to Parliament for a family borough. He remained in Parliament until 1768, an exceptionally well-informed member not without influence behind the scenes.

His father died in 1745, having secured for him lucrative places in the Exchequer and Custom House that gave him a generous income for life. He never married.

In 1747 he moved to Strawberry Hill, Twickenham, eleven miles from his London house in Arlington Street; he began remodelling it with Gothic embellishments in 1749. The Strawberry Hill Press, the first private press in England, opened in 1757 with Gray's Pindaric Odes.

Walpole's versatility as a writer appears in his essays, political pamphlets, verse, and seven works that were highly regarded in his own day and have not been forgotten in ours. They were (1) *Aedes Walpolianae* (a catalogue of his father's great collection of pictures), 1747; (2) *A Catalogue of the Royal and Noble Authors of England*, 2 vols, 1758; (3) *Fugitive Pieces in Verse and Prose*, 1758; (4) *Anecdotes of Painting in England* and *A Catalogue of Engravers*, 5 vols, 1762–71; (5) *The Castle of Otranto*, 1765; (6) *Historic Doubts on the Life and Reign of King Richard III*, 1768; (7) *The Mysterious Mother* (a tragedy), 1768. Numbers 2, 3, 4, and 7 were printed at Strawberry Hill; all but 3 and 7 were pioneer works, the first of their kind in England. Walpole planned his *Works of Horatio Walpole, Earl of Orford*, 5 vols, which appeared in 1798, the year after his death; in it was the first selection of his letters. He began writing his *Memoirs* in 1751 and continued them until 1791. Like his letters, they are a major source for eighteenth-century studies and were also published posthumously.

Walpole succeeded his nephew in 1791 as fourth Earl of Orford, but never took his seat in the House of Lords.

During the last forty years of his life he suffered from periodic attacks of gout, which he bore with fortitude and resignation.

He died 2 March 1797 in his eightieth year.

Walpole's Chief Correspondents in the Order of Their Appearance Here

The Rev. William Cole (1714–82), an Eton and King's contemporary, was Walpole's favourite correspondent about English antiquities. Volumes 1 and 2. Walpole's 178 letters to Cole are in the British Museum; Cole's 186 letters to Walpole are in the Victoria and Albert Museum, London.

Mme la Marquise du Deffand (1696–1780), whom Walpole described as 'an old blind *débauchée* of wit' when he met her in 1765, was a notable letter-writer in her own right. Walpole made four subsequent trips to Paris expressly to see her. Volumes 2 to 8. Her 841 letters to him are mostly in the Bodleian Library, Oxford; the seven surviving letters from him to her are in the Lewis Walpole Library at Farmington, Connecticut; the rest were destroyed after Walpole's death, presumably by his order, but copies of many fragments have been printed.

George Montagu (ca 1713–80), one of Walpole's closest friends at Eton. He lived in the country, becoming so idle that he finally gave up writing altogether ten years before he died. Volumes 9 and 10. Walpole's 262 letters deal mainly with his social life.

Miss Mary Berry (1763–1852) and Miss Agnes Berry (1764–1851) added much to Walpole's old age. He moved them and their father to the cottage on his property in which he had established Kitty Clive on her retirement from the stage and which he called 'Cliveden' in her honour. The Berrys lived there until Walpole died in 1797. Mary, whom he made his literary executrix, brought out his *Works* in five volumes, quarto, the following year, and until her death fifty-four years later was his champion against hostile critics such as Macaulay. Volumes 11 and 12. Walpole's 164 letters (all but eight of which are to Mary) are mostly in the Pierpont Morgan Library. All but eleven of the sisters' letters to him have disappeared.

Thomas Gray (1716–71), the poet, one of Walpole's closest friends at Eton and Cambridge, was taken by Walpole on his Grand Tour, 1739–41. They parted company after two years of travel, but were reconciled later. Walpole had much to do with the publication of Gray's poems and Gray helped him in his antiquarian ventures. Gray destroyed all but thirteen of

Walpole's letters to him, but Walpole kept Gray's letters. Volumes 13 and 14. Most of the originals of Gray's 126 letters are at Pembroke College, Cambridge; Walpole's are in the Lewis Walpole Library.

Sir Horace Mann, Bt (1706–86), was the British diplomatic representative from 1738 to 1786 at Florence, where he was Walpole's and Gray's host for a year on their Grand Tour. Walpole and he never met again, but for forty-five years they corresponded regularly. Foreign affairs predominate in their letters. Volumes 17 to 27. Walpole got his letters back from Mann and copied them, with the assistance of his printer-secretary, Thomas Kirgate (1734–1810), into six folio volumes, two of which are shown in this exhibition (Nos. 20 and 23). The originals were later destroyed, presumably on Walpole's order. Mann's letters to Walpole are also in the Lewis Walpole Library. The correspondence totals 1,724 letters that average perhaps 1,000 words each.

The Rev. William Mason (1725–97), highly regarded in his day as a poet, is better known now as Gray's biographer. He succeeded Gray as the recipient of Walpole's letters on contemporary literature. As time went on the chief subject of the correspondence became political and ended in coolness. Volumes 28 and 29. Most of Walpole's 216 letters to Mason have disappeared; Mason's 116 letters to Walpole are in the Lewis Walpole Library.

The Hon. Anne Liddell (ca 1738–1804) first married the 3d Duke of Grafton, and after she was divorced by him, the 2d Earl of Upper Ossory, by whom she had had a daughter. She succeeded Montagu as the recipient of Walpole's reports on the great world. Volumes 32 to 34. Walpole's letters to her, 450 in number, were acquired by their first editor, Vernon Smith, and descended to the late Robert Vernon of Taunton, Somerset, whose son owns them; only one of her letters to Walpole has been found.

John Chute (1701–76) of the Vyne, Hampshire, and Richard Bentley (1708–81), members of the Committee that redesigned Strawberry Hill in the Gothic manner. Volume 35. Of the fifty letters in the Chute correspondence, over half are in the Lewis Walpole Library; the rest are missing. Thirty-six of Walpole's letters to Bentley were printed in Walpole's *Works,* but the originals and Bentley's replies have disappeared.

Field Marshal the Hon. Henry Seymour Conway (1719–95), his wife Lady Ailesbury (1721–1803), and Conway's brother, 1st Earl and 1st Marquess of Hertford (1718–94). Volumes 37 to 39. Conway and Hertford were Walpole's first cousins on his mother's side. Walpole's concern for Conway's welfare—his marriage and political career—was that of a slightly older and devoted brother. One is closer to Walpole in this correspondence than in any other. Of the 372 letters, over half are at Farmington; most of the rest are missing; virtually all forty of the letters to and from Lady Ailesbury are in the Lewis Walpole Library. Only thirty-eight of Walpole's letters to Hertford have been printed and of them nearly all are missing; 178 of Hertford's letters to Walpole are in the British Museum.

In the Yale Walpole there will be some 7,500 letters, rather more than half from Walpole, of which about 6,500 have been printed from the originals or photostats of them. The missing thousand are those from Walpole that have been lost sight of for over a hundred years.

How many unrecorded letters there are in existence we have of course no idea. The sole list of his letters that Walpole kept appears in his Paris Journals and is published in our Volume 7. Of the letters mentioned in it only about a third have turned up. Four large correspondences have almost totally disappeared: those with Conway's and Lady Ailesbury's daughter, who became Mrs Damer; with Lady Ailesbury's son-in-law, the 3d Duke of Richmond; with Walpole's half-sister Lady Mary Churchill; and with Lady Mary's husband. During the past forty years caches of new letters in the correspondence have been discovered in Somerset, Buckinghamshire, Nottinghamshire, South Africa, and Ceylon. Another may be found next Tuesday and necessitate supplementary volumes to the Yale Walpole. Let us hope so.

1. Walpole's Notebook, 1786

This is the last of Walpole's three notebooks, which he dated 1759, 1771, and 1786. In them he recorded his journeys to country houses, notes for a fifth volume of his *Anecdotes of Painting in England,* notes on Shakespeare and extracts from his reading, notes on the streets of London, court anecdotes, charades, riddles, epigrams, epitaphs, etc., and, under 'Miscellaneous,' such entries as, 'I believe it is little known that Archbishop Abbot ever wrote English verses,' with many cuttings from newspapers, which he dated. Only the journeys to country houses, notes on painting in England, and notes on Shakespeare have been printed, but these notebooks have been drawn on extensively in the Yale Walpole and the Hazen catalogue of Walpole's library. Walpole called the first two 'Books of Materials,' this last one, 'Miscellany.' He used them in writing his works and letters.

The seal became his bookplate after he succeeded his nephew as Earl of Orford in 1791. The epigraph from Colley Cibber's *Apology* marks his preoccupation with us, posterity: '—such remaining scraps as may not perhaps be worth the reader's notice: but if they are such as tempt me to write them, why may not I hope that in this wide world there may be many an idle soul no wiser than myself, who may be equally tempted to read them?'

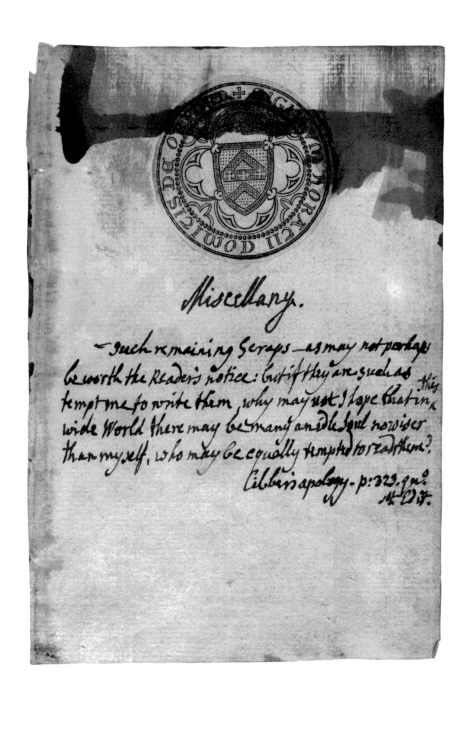

Miscellany.

— such remaining Scraps — as may not perhaps
be worth the Reader's notice: but if they are such as
tempt me to write them, why may not I hope that in this a
wide World there may be many an idle Soul no wiser
than myself, who may be equally tempted to read them?

Cibber's apology - p: 323. 9n°
M.D.F.

2. Walpole's Copy of *The Castle of Otranto*, 1765, Presented to William Cole

Volume 1, page 85. Walpole wrote Cole, 28 February 1765: 'If you will tell me how to send it, and are partial enough to me to read a profane work in the style of former centuries, I shall convey to you a little story-book, which I published some time ago, though not boldly with my own name; but it has succeeded so well, that I do not any longer entirely keep the secret: does the title, *The Castle of Otranto,* tempt you?' Cole copied this passage and the one on *The Castle of Otranto* in Walpole's letter of 9 March 1765 in his copy.

Over a hundred editions of the novel have been published in England, America, France, Germany, Italy, and Russia. Of these, fourteen have appeared in this century, including one at Leningrad in 1967 of 50,000 copies. The most beautiful *Otranto* is the one printed by Bodoni at Parma for J. Edwards of London in 1791. See No. 48 for Walpole's copy of it.

THE

CASTLE of OTRANTO,

A

S T O R Y.

Translated by

WILLIAM MARSHAL, Gent.

From the Original ITALIAN of

ONUPHRIO MURALTO,

CANON of the Church of St. NICHOLAS
at OTRANTO.

LONDON:

Printed for THO. LOWNDS in Fleet-Street.
MDCCLXV.

3. Paul Sandby's View of the East and South Fronts of Strawberry Hill, ca 1783

Volume 2, page 245. Walpole to Cole, 24 November 1780: 'I endeavoured to give our antiquaries a little wrench towards taste—but it was in vain. Sandby and our engravers of views have lent them a great deal—but there it stops.' Paul Sandby (1725–1809) is the best known of 'the painters of views' Walpole employed at Strawberry Hill. This view shows the completed main building. The east portion was finished in 1754 (another view of it appears in No. 52) and may be attributed largely to Bentley. The Great Cloister to the west and the Gallery above it owe much to Chute. Sandby's water-colour was engraved as a folding plate for Walpole's *Description of Strawberry Hill*, 1784.

4. Mme du Deffand's Letter in the Name of Mme de Sévigné

Volume 3, page 51. The letter shown was sent in a white and gold snuff-box (now in the possession of Lord Waldegrave) with a miniature of Mme de Sévigné on its lid and the cipher of Rabutin and Sévigné on the bottom. The account of how the French ambassador, Comte de Guerchy, smuggled it and the letter into Walpole's Arlington Street house and Walpole's mystification and fear of being ridiculous is told in W. S. Lewis, 'Horace Walpole's Letter from Madame de Sévigné,' Farmington, Conn., 1933.

The letter reads in part: 'Des Champs Élisées; point de succession de temps, point de date. Je connais votre folle passion pour moi, votre enthousiasme pour mes lettres, votre vénération pour les lieux que j'ai habités; j'ai appris le culte que vous m'y avez rendu; j'en suis si pénétrée que j'ai sollicité et obtenu la permission de mes souveraines de vous venir trouver pour ne vous quitter jamais; j'abandonne sans regret ces lieux fortunés, je vous préfère à tous ses habitants. . . .

Rabutin de Sévigné'

Des champs Elisées; point de succession de
tems point de date

Je connois votre folle passion pour moi, votre
enthousiasme pour mes lettres, votre veneration
pour les lieux que j'ai habités; j'ai appris le culte
que vous m'avez rendu, j'en suis si penetrée
que j'ai sollicité et obtenu la permission de
mes souverains de vous venir trouver pour ne
vous quitter jamais, j'abandonne sans regret
ces lieux fortunés, je vous préfere a tous les
habitans, jouissez du plaisir de me voir, ne
vous plaignez point que ce ne soit qu'en
peinture, c'est la seule existence que puissent
avoir les ombres. J'ai été maîtresse de choisir
l'âge ou je voulois reparoître, j'ai pris celui
de vingt cinq ans pour m'assurer d'être toujours
pour vous un objet agreable, ne craignez aucun
changement, c'est un singulier avantage des
ombres, quoi que legeres elles sont immuables.

J'ai pris la plus petitte figure qu'il m'a
été possible pour n'être jamais séparée de vous,
je veux vous accompagner par tout, sur terre,

5. Louis XVI's Translation of Walpole's

Historic Doubts of the Life and Reign of Richard III

Volume 4, page 11. Mme du Deffand describes her difficulty in finding someone to translate Walpole's *Historic Doubts*. She never did find a translator, and no French edition of the book appeared until 1800, twenty years after she died. Its translator was Louis XVI who worked on this manuscript while in the Tuileries. Walpole, who agonized over the sufferings of the King and Queen, died three years before the translation was published, and consequently never knew that he had indirectly eased the King's last days. See No. 55.

à Londres
chez J. Dodsley
dans le ~~fort mall~~
1768

Doutes historiques sur la vie et le regne de Richard III.
par Mr Horace Walpole.

L'histoire n'est fondée que sur le temoignage des auteurs qui nous l'ont transmise. Il importe donc extremement, pour la bien scavoir, de bien connoitre quels ont été ces auteurs. Rien n'est à negliger sur ce point; le temps ou ils ont vecu, leur naissance, leur patrie, la part qu'ils ont eu aux affaires, les moyens par lesquels ils ont été instruits, et l'interest qu'ils y pouvoient prendre, sont des circonstances essentielles qu'il n'est pas permis d'ignorer; de la depend le plus ou moins d'autorité qu'ils doivent avoir: et sans cette connoissance, on court risque tres souvent de prendre pour guide un historien de mauvaise foy, ou du moins mal informé.

Hist. de l'Academie des Inscriptions Vol. X.

Preface

La pluspart des historiens sont si incompetans pour le sujet qu'ils ~~entreprennent~~ *embrassent*, ~~incertain qui~~ *si incertain qu'on ne scauroit* mettre en doute, si les moeurs des temps passés ~~renversent~~ *remontent*, qu'ils ~~fussent~~ *soient* été capables de connoitre les evenements de leur propre temps, ~~comme~~ *de la maniere* ils nous sont transmis par l'ignorance et la mauvaise ~~representation~~. Toute l'histoire ~~fort anciennes sont de veritables fables, excepte celle des juifs eclairés par l'esprit saint; excepte celle des gens illuminés~~ ~~est une~~ *fable parfaite.* Elle a ~~été écrite~~ par des ~~Poetes, et ressemble~~ ~~d'après~~ ~~selon leurs rapports~~, et calculée seulement pour donner une bonne idée de l'origine de chaque nation. Les Dieux et les demi Dieux sont les principaux acteurs, et on doit s'attendre ~~dans une histoire~~ *personnages* surement de trouver la verité, ou les acteurs sont nos auteurs. Les historiens Grecs n'ont d'avantage, sur les ~~anciens~~, que par la beauté de leur langage, ~~ou par ce qu'elles~~ *aux* nous est plus familiere. Menyo capac le fils du soleil est aussi surement ~~forcé~~ *la tige* d'une maison ~~sans~~ Royalle, que l'ancien des Heraclides. ~~qu'il~~ *a qu'elle verité, doit on s'attendre* ~~replie faut on attendre~~ a la verité quand l'identité des personnes ~~meme~~ est incertaine? les actions d'une personne sont attribuées a plusieurs, et celles de plusieurs a une. On ne scait pas si il n'y a eu qu'un seul Hercule ou s'il y en a eu vingt.

6. Walpole's Copy of the Strawberry Hill *Grammont*, 1772

Volume 5, page 217. Mme du Deffand to Walpole, 14 April 1772. When he asked her if he might dedicate the Strawberry edition of Grammont's *Memoirs* to her, she replied: 'Venons à l'honneur que vous voulez me faire: il n'est pas douteux que je n'y sois bien sensible; mais mon amour-propre ne m'aveugle pas au point de consentir que vous me nommiez, il suffit qu'on me devine, en voilà assez pour ma gloire.' Nevertheless, Walpole identified her in his own copy (Hazen 2511).

A

MADAME -----

Marie de Vichi
Marquise du Deffand.

L'Editeur vous confacre cette Edition,
comme un monument de fon Amitié,
de fon Admiration, & de fon Refpect ; à
Vous, dont les Graces, l'Efprit, & le Goût
retracent au fiecle prefent le fiecle de Louis
quatorze & les agremens de l'Auteur de
ces Memoires.

7.   Walpole to Mme du Deffand, 13 January 1775

Volume 6, page 135. One of his six letters to her that have survived. The rest were apparently destroyed by his order after Miss Berry had used them in her edition of Mme du Deffand's letters to him.

En toute verité je vous assure que je n'ai pas pensé à vous
faire des menaces. Je vous ai dit en badinant que je ne
voulois vous ecrire de huit jours — & voila ou me fait tomber
le malheur de ne pas ecrire dans ma propre langue. Si je
ne parle pas toujours d'un serieux phlegmatique, votre
mefiance naturelle vous fait soupçonner que je suis de mau=
vaise humeur — je ne sçais pas de remede, il faut se soumettre
à ces contretems. au moins vous voyez que je ne me fache pas au=
=jourd'hui.

Non, assurement, Mon Cousin ne gardera pas votre Madame de
Prie. Vous me l'aviez offert, & je n'ai pas voulu vous l'oter — mais
puisque vous la donnez, je pretends qu'elle est à moi comme plus
ancien en date. Ne vous donnez plus de peine sur Madame
D'Olonne; vous en avez deja trop pris. Je vous prie seulement
de me la faire acheter à la vente, si le prix ne passe pas cent
Louis ou environ, ce qui seroit bien payer sa fantaisie; mais
j'ai peur que je ne l'aurai pas. Il y a un Mons.r d'Henin ou bien
d'Henin, demeurant dans la meme rue avec le Chevalier
Lambert, & tout pres de l'hotel de Richelieu, & qui achete à tort
& à travers tous les ouvrages soi disants de Petitot, qui me
l'emportera, & j'en serai faché. Il y avoit encore un monsieur

8. Snuff-Box with Tonton's Portrait

Volume 7, page 2. Mme du Deffand wrote Walpole, 6 January 1778: 'Deux jours après cette facétie, la Maréchale m'apporta mes étrennes, elle mit sur mes genoux les six derniers in-quarto de Voltaire sur lesquels il y avait un petit sac dans lequel il y avait une très jolie boîte d'or et le portrait de Tonton; ainsi elle me donnait Voltaire et mon chien, et voici le couplet qui y était joint:

> Vous les trouvez tous deux charmants,
> Nous les trouvons tous deux mordants;
>   Voilà la ressemblance:
> L'un ne mord que ses ennemis,
> Et l'autre mord tous vos amis,
>   Voilà la différence.

Ce couplet est du Chevalier de Boufflers.'

She bequeathed Tonton (who bit friends as long as he lived) and the snuff-box to Walpole. When Tonton arrived Walpole wrote Mason 22 May 1781: 'You will find that I have gotten a new idol, in a word, a successor to Rosette and almost as great a favourite, nor is this a breach of vows and constancy, but an act of piety. In a word, my poor dear old friend Madame du Deffand had a little dog of which she was extremely fond, and the last time I saw her she made me promise if I should survive her to take charge of it. I did. It is arrived and I was going to say, it is incredible how fond I am of it, but I have no occasion to brag of my dogmanity. I dined at Richmond House t'other day, and mentioning whither I was going, the Duke said, "Own the truth, shall not you call at home first and see Tonton?" He guessed rightly. He is now sitting on my paper as I write—not the Duke, but Tonton.'

9.   Walpole's 'Portrait' of Mme du Deffand, 1766

Volume 8, page 55.   Where do Wit and Memory dwell?
                     Where is Fancy's favourite cell? . . .
The Portrait was written in response to Mme du Deffand's request in her
letter of 30 November 1766. Walpole pasted this copy of her 'Portrait' in
the 'Recueil de divers ouvrages,' which Mme du Deffand bequeathed him
(Hazen 2545).

Portrait
de Madame la Marquise du Deffand,
1766.

Where do Wit and Memory dwell?
Where is Fancy's favourite Cell?
Where does Judgment hold her court,
And dictate laws to Mirth and sport?
Where does Reason — not the Dame,
Who arrogates the Sage's name,
And proud of self-conferr'd degree,
Esteems herself Philosophy?
But the Reason that I mean,
The slave of truth & passion's Queen,
Who doubts, not dictates; seeks the best,
And to Presumption leaves the rest;
With whom resides the winning Fair?
With Rousseau? — no; nor with Voltaire,
Nor where leaf-gold of Eloquence,
Adorning less than veiling Sense,
Dazzles the passions It can heat,
And makes them party to the cheat.
Where does Patience, tell who know,
Bear irremediable woe,
And, tho of life's best joy bereft,
Smile on the little portion left?
Lastly tell, where boundless flows
The richest stream that Friendship knows!

10. Newstead Abbey by J. C. Barrow, 1793

Volume 9, page 299. Walpole wrote Montagu, 1 September 1760: 'As I returned, I saw Newstead and Althorpe; I like both. The former is the very abbey. The great east window of the church remains, and connects with the house; the hall entire, the refectory entire, the cloister untouched with the ancient cistern of the convent and their arms on it, a private chapel quite perfect.' Walpole recorded his visit to Newstead in his 'Book of Materials, 1759': 'August 1760: Newstede, the Convent, much as it was; the West Window remaining in an arch close to the House. . . . conduit before the House. The Hall, with vaulted roof unpainted, remaining.' Walpole had many drawings by J. C. Barrow.

Newstead, which belonged to the Byrons, was described by the poet under the name of 'Norman Abbey' in *Don Juan,* canto 13, stanzas LIX–LXVII. Byron was a champion of Walpole in the new century. 'It is the fashion to underrate Horace Walpole,' he wrote in the Preface to *Marino Faliero,* 1821, 'firstly, because he was a nobleman, and secondly, because he was a gentleman; but to say nothing of the composition of his incomparable letters, and of the *Castle of Otranto,* he is the "Ultimus Romanorum," the author of the *Mysterious Mother,* a tragedy of the highest order, and not a puling love-play. He is the father of the first romance, and of the last tragedy in our language, and surely worthy of a higher place than any living writer, be he who he may.'

Volume 10, page 314. This letter to Montagu of 7 July 1770 is one of Walpole's great set-pieces. It records the house-party at Stowe that Lord and Lady Temple gave for Princess Amelia, George III's aunt.

The illustrations are from *Stowe: A Description of the Magnificent House and Gardens of the Right Honourable Richard Grenville Temple, Earl Temple . . . Embellished with a General Plan of the Gardens, and also a separate Plan of each Building, with Prospective Views of the same,* and it is possible that Walpole took this copy of it (Hazen 2387:4) with him. The Gothic Temple and Palladian Bridge are shown. Walpole's note on the latter reads: 'This was originally closed up on one side with paintings in which was Fame drawing a veil over the reign of George 2d, but this was taken away on Lord Temple's coming into place' and before Princess Amelia, George II's daughter, went to Stowe on the house-party.

On the Right-hand are Ladies, employing themselves in Needle and Shell-work.—On the opposite Side, are Ladies diverting themselves with Painting and Music.

The *Gothic* Temple,

is a large Building of red Stone, 70 Feet high, upon a rising Ground, adorned in the Gothic Way with carved Work and painted Glass. The Disposition within is very beautiful. You enter a circular Room, the Dome of which is ornamented with the Descents of the *Temple* Family. On the second Story, is a Gallery: The Tower affords a very extensive View round the Country. *It was designed by Gibbs.*

The Hill round the Temple is adorned with very good Statues, by *Rysbrack*, of the seven *Saxon* Deities, who gave Names to the Days of the Week.—The Portico of the Temple of *Concord* and *Victory* has a beautiful Effect from this Place.

The *Palladian* Bridge,

The Roof of which is supported by *Ionic* Pillars. From hence you pass into the great Terras-walk, which is 3000 Feet long.

The Temple of Friendship,

is a large Structure of the *Doric* Order. On the Outside is this Motto:

Amicitiæ S.———Sacred to Friendship.

The Inside is furnished with the Busts of the late Viscount *Cobham* and his Friends, *viz. Frederick* Prince of *Wales*; the Earls of *Chesterfield*, *Westmoreland*, and *Marchmont*; the Lords *Cobham*, *Gower*, and *Bathurst*; *Richard Grenville*, now Earl *Temple*; *William Pitt*, now Earl of *Chatham*, and *George Lyttleton*, now Lord *Lyttleton*.

The

This was originally closed up on one side with paintings, in which frame drewing a veil over the reign of George 2d, but this was taken away at Lord Temple's coming into place.

The Gothic Temple.

The Palladian Bridge.

B. Seeley delin.
G. L. Smith sculp.

12. Little Strawberry Hill or Cliveden

by Mary Berry

Volume 11, page 267. Walpole wrote Mary Berry at Florence, 19 May 1791: 'You are learning perspective to take views; I am glad; can one have too many resources in one's self?'

Miss Berry wrote on the back of the sketch, 'Little Strawberry Hill M. Berry,' using the cottage's original name instead of 'Cliveden,' which is what Walpole called it after he established Kitty Clive there on her retirement from the stage. Agnes Berry is shown on 'her' balcony.

13. The Garden at Little Strawberry Hill

(Cliveden)

by J. C. Barrow, 1791

Volume 12, page 120. Walpole to Mary Berry, 1 October 1794: 'I . . . returned by Cliveden to look after your new plant-shed, and took Mrs Richardson into the garden with me. It is quite finished except glazing, and the garden is as trim as that in Milton's *Allegro,* and much prettier, though not so immortal.'

Walpole pasted these drawings in his extra-illustrated copy of *A Description of Strawberry Hill,* 1784 (Hazen 3582). The notes are by Thomas Kirgate, his printer-secretary for nearly thirty years. The note on the upper drawing is, 'Cliveden near Strawberry Hill, Twickenham, formerly the villa of Mrs Catherine Clive the comedian, and now of Miss Mary and Miss Agnes Berry, 1792.'

14.   The First Page of Walpole's 'Short Notes'

of His Life

Volume 13, page 3. Walpole began writing this summary account of himself about 1750 and continued it until 1779, his sixty-second year. Most of it was first printed by Richard Bentley, the publisher of Walpole's letters to Mann, 1843–44, and reprinted by Peter Cunningham in his edition of Walpole's *Letters,* 1857, and by Mrs Toynbee in 1903. The deletions made by the first editor have been restored in the Yale Walpole. It is perhaps the most important Walpole manuscript in existence.

Short Notes
of the life of
Horatio Walpole
youngest Son of
Sr Robert Walpole Earl of Orford
and of
Catherine Shorter, his first Wife.

I was born in Arlington street near
St James's London Sept. 24. 1717. O.S. my
Godfathers were Charles Fitzroy Duke of
Grafton, & my Uncle Horatio Walpole;
My Godmother, my Aunt, Dorothy Lady
Viscountess Townshend.

I was inoculated for the
small pox in 1724.

In 1725 I went to Bexley in Kent with
my cousins the four younger sons of
Lord Townshend & with a Tutor, Edward
Weston, one of the sons of Stephen Bishop
of Exeter, & continued there some months.
The next summer, I had the same education
at Twickenham, Middlesex.; & the
intervening winters I went every day
to study under mr Weston at Ld Townshend's.
April 26. 1727. I went to Eton school,
where mr Henry Bland, (since Prebendary
of Durham) eldest son of Dr Henry Bland,
master of the school, & since Provost of Eton
& Dean of Durham, was my Tutor.

Lincolnshire
v. next page.

+ I left Eton school Sept. 23. 1734: and
march 11th 1735 went to King's college.
Cambridge. My public Tutor was mr John
Smith; my private mr Anstey, afterwards
mr John Whaley was my Tutor. I went to
lectures in civil law to Dr Dickins of
Trinityhall. to mathematical lectures to
blind Professor Saunderson, for a short time:
afterwards mr Trevigar read lectures to me
in mathematics & philosophy. I heard Dr
Battie's anatomical lectures. I had learned
French at Eton; I learned Italian at Cambridge
of Signor Piazza. at home I learned to dance
& fence; & to draw of Bernard Lens, master
to the Duke & Princesses.

15. A Copy of Watteau, by Walpole, 1737

At the end of the first page of Walpole's 'Short Notes' of his life (No. 14), Walpole says that he 'learned . . . to draw of Bernard Lens, Master to the Duke [of Cumberland] and Princesses.' Walpole signed this drawing and dated it 1737 when he was in his twentieth year. He hung it in his bedroom at Strawberry Hill.

16. Gray's and Bentley's Drawings of Stoke House

for Gray's 'Long Story'

17. Grignion's Engraving of Bentley's Drawing

Volume 14, page 59. Walpole recorded in 'Short Notes' of his life under 1753, 'This year I published [through Dodsley in London] a fine edition of six poems of Mr T. Gray, with prints from designs of Mr R. Bentley.' The work is regarded now as a milestone in English book illustration.

In the copy at the top (Hazen 3698), Walpole pasted Bentley's drawings that are still mistaken for prints. It is open to the head-piece of 'A Long Story' and to Gray's sketch of Stoke House, the seat of the poem, which Gray sent to Walpole 8 July 1752 with the note, 'Mr Bentley (I believe) will catch a better idea of Stoke House from any old barn he sees, than from my sketch, but I will try my skill.' Walpole's note reads, 'Mr Gray's original sketch of Stoke from which Mr Bentley made the drawing that is engraved.' Below (No. 17) is Walpole's copy of the published book (Hazen 2044), open at Grignion's engraving of Bentley's rendering of Gray's sketch. Walpole's note identifying Grignion as the engraver is at the lower left.

Mr Gray's original Sketch of Stoke from which Mr Bentley made the drawing that is engraved.

Volume 15, page 316. The drawing is in pencil on paper, 9½ x 7¾ inches. It is inscribed, 'This is by George Dance from the collection of Miss M. Dance, his great granddaughter.'

Joseph Farington wrote in his *Diary:* 'Saturday July 13 [1793]. Went early this morning in company with Mr George Dance, the architect, and Mr Samuel Lysons of the Temple, to Lord Orford's at Strawberry Hill, where we breakfasted with his Lordship. In the forenoon Mr Dance made a drawing from his Lordship's profile, an excellent resemblance. Lord Orford is now in his 76th year, infirm in his body, but lively and attentive in mind.' Another drawing of Walpole by Dance, slightly smaller than this one, is in the National Portrait Gallery, London.

H. Walpole   Earl of Oxford

19. Walpole Charged with Chatterton's Death

Volume 16, page 345. The editor of Chatterton's *Miscellanies in Prose and Verse*, 1778, wrote on page xviii, 'One of his [Chatterton's] first efforts, to emerge from a situation so irksome to him, was an application to a gentleman well known in the republic of letters; which unfortunately for the public, and himself, met with a very cold reception; and which the disappointed author always spoke of with a high degree of acrimony, whenever it was mentioned to him.' In his copy (Hazen 3690), Walpole has identified himself as the 'gentleman well known in the republic of letters.'

Wordsworth, Coleridge, Hazlitt, and many others sided with Chatterton. To them he was

the marvellous boy,
The sleepless soul that perished in his pride.

No one regretted his early death more than Walpole. The full account of his honourable dealings with Chatterton appears in his correspondence and is now generally accepted.

warmth, which the excellence of his author
might have been expected to excite; surely,
that excellence demanded some few words
of commendation : it is also to be lamented
that he did not enter more minutely into
the disposition and circumstances of one
whom he could not but respect as an author,
however he might dislike his character,
as a man : and here it must be confessed,
Chatterton appears to us in the most un-
favourable point of view. He possessed all
the vices and irregularities of youth, and
his profligacy was, at least, as conspicuous
as his abilities. Although he was of a profession which might be said to accelerate
his pursuits in antiquities, yet so averse
was he to that profession, that he could never overcome it. One of his first efforts,
to emerge from a situation so irksome to
Mr. H. Walpole him, was an application to a gentleman
well known in the republic of letters;
which

20.   Walpole's Title-Page to the

Mann Correspondence

Volume 17, page 1. The epigraph from Pliny the Elder, 'Will this be of any interest to posterity. I wonder!' reflects Walpole's life-long preoccupation with posterity. The title-page is in his hand of the late 1740s when he got back the first batch of his letters from Mann and began transcribing them.

A
Collection
of
Letters
from
Horace Walpole
Youngest Son of Sr Robert Walpole
Earl of Orford
to
Horace Mann
Resident at Florence
from
King George the Second:
transcribed from the Originals.

Vol: 1.st

Posteris an aliqua cura, nescio!
Plin. epist.

Volume 18, pages 166–67. Walpole wrote Mann, 13 Feb. 1743 OS: 'I must tell you an amusing scene I had with him [Lord Lincoln] last week. You know he is just made lord of the Bedchamber; and you must know too that his general style of talking is the vigorous—T'other night at supper at the Duchess of Richmond's, he said to Lady Albemarle, "but why won't Lord Bury write to wish me joy?" "Why," said she, "to be sure he does not know it." "Pho, not know it, why all the world must know it!" The next night happened to be the masquerade night: we were all to go together from the Duchess's. I dressed myself in an Indian dress, and after he was come thither, walked into the room, made him three low bows, and kneeling down, took a letter out of my bosom, wrapped in Persian silk, and laid it on my head: he stared violently! They persuaded him to take it: it was a Persian letter from Kouli Kan, and was written on a long sheet of red Indian paper—here it is:

> Thomas Kouli Kan Schah Nadir
> to Henry Clinton Earl of Lincoln.

Highly favoured *among women*.

  'Yesterday's sun brought us the glad tidings of the high post to which thou hast been advanced by our brother the Sultan of the Western Isles. . . . We would know of thee what is the nature of thy new post. Does thy admission to the bedchamber of thy Lord give thee access to his women? Or are they veiled from thy sight as ours in Persia?

  'Most potent Lord, we have sent thee as a mark of our grace fifty of the most beautiful maidens of Persia, fifty more of Georgia, and fifty of the most chosen of Circassia. . . . Adieu! Happy young man! May thy days be as long as thy manhood . . . and when thou art full of years, may Azraël the angel of death conduct thee to those fields of light, where the favourites of the Prophet taste eternal joys in the arms of the beautiful houris!

>   From the Seraglio of Ispahan, the first of the month Regeb.'

Most Potent Lord, We have sent Thee, as a Mark of our Grace, Fifty of the most Beautifull Maidens of Persia, Fifty more of Georgia, and Fifty of the most Chosen of Circassia. Moreover, having heard that there are no Eunuchs in thy Country, but a few which you buy in a Neighbouring Kingdom at an Excessive Price, and considering what Occasion thy Magnificence must have for them to guard the pro-digious Number of Women in thy Seraglio; We have sent Thee a Thousand Black Eunuchs.

Adieu! Happy Young Man! May Thy Days be as long as thy Manhood, and may Thy Manhood, continue more Piercing than Zufager, That Sword of Hali, which had Two Points. And when Thou art full of years, may Azrael the Angel of Death, conduct Thee to Those Fields of Light, where the Favourites of the Prophet taste Eternal Joys in the Arms of the Beautifull Houries!

From the Seraglio of Ispahan
The first of the Moon Regeb.

22. Sir Robert Walpole's Last Words

Volume 19, page 24. Walpole writes Mann, 29 March 1745 OS, that he cannot talk about his father's death. He had been in constant attendance upon him during his last illness and was physically and emotionally exhausted. Shown here is his transcript of Sir Robert's last words:

'Dr Horace This Lixivium has blown me up. 2. It has tore me to pieces. The Affair is over with me; that it may be short Dr Ranby, is all I desire. Give me more opium; knock me down. I expect nothing but to have ease. Dr Horace if one must die, tis hard to die in pain.

'Why do ye all stand round me! are ye all waiting there, because this is the last night.

'Insisted on Ranby's telling Him if he shd die before morning: Ranby gave him no hopes: he then talk'd in private with Ranby; then a quarter of an hour just before three with Ld Walpole. afterwards again with Ranby. To Ranby, Tis Impossible not to be a little disturbed at going out of the world, but you see I am not afraid.'

Dr Horace This lixivium has blown
me up. 2. It has tore me to peices.
the Affair is over with me; that it
may be short Dr Hawky, is all I desire.
Give me more Opeium; knock me down.
I expect nothing but to have ease.
Dr Horace if one must die, tis hard
to die in pain.
Why do ye all stand round me! are
ye all waiting here, because this
is the last night.
Insisted on Hawky's telling him if he
shd die before morning: Hawky gave
him no hopes: he then talk'd in private
with Hawky; then a quarter of an hour
just before three wth D Walpole. after
wards again wth Hawky. To Hawky, Tis
Impossible not to be a little disturbd at
going out of the world, but you see I am
not afraid.

23.   Serendipity

24.   The Book of Venetian Arms

Volume 20, page 407. Walpole thanked Mann, 28 January 1754, for his gift of a portrait of Bianca Cappello (1548–87), mistress and wife of Francesco I, Grand Duke of Tuscany. Walpole planned a frame for her 'with the grand-ducal coronet at top, her story on a label at bottom, which Gray is to compose in Latin . . . the Medici arms on one side, and the Capello's on the other. I must tell you a critical discovery of mine *à propos:* in an old book of Venetian arms, there are two coats of Capello, who from their *name* bear a *hat,* on one of them is added a flower-de-luce on a blue ball, which I am persuaded was given to the family by the Great Duke, in consideration of this alliance; the Medicis you know bore such a badge at the top of their own arms; this discovery I made by a talisman, which Mr Chute calls the *sortes Walpolianae,* by which I find everything I want *à point nommé* wherever I dip for it. This discovery indeed is almost of that kind which I call *serendipity,* a very expressive word, which as I have nothing better to tell you, I shall endeavour to explain to you: you will understand it better by the derivation than by the definition. I once read a silly fairy tale, called *The Three Princes of Serendip:* as their highnesses travelled, they were always making discoveries, by accidents and sagacity, of things which they were not in quest of: for instance, one of them discovered that a mule blind of the right eye had travelled the same road lately, because the grass was eaten only on the left side, where it was worse than on the right—now do you understand *serendipity?'*

The 'old book of Venetian arms' (No. 24) is *Le arme overo insegne di tutti li nobili . . . di Venetia,* Venice, 1578 (Hazen 2051). It is open at the arms of the Cappellos. Walpole made the pencilled cross at the left.

164.

bespeak & have executed such an Inscription!) the Medici-arms on one side, & the Capello's on the other. I must tell you a critical discovery of mine apropos: in an old book of Venetian arms, there are two coats of Capello, who from their name bear a hat, on one of them is added a flowerdeluce on a blue ball, which I am persuaded was given to the family by the Great Duke, in consideration of this alliance; the Medicis you know bore such a badge at the top of their own arms: This discovery I made by a talisman, which Mr Chute calls the sortes Walpolianæ; by which I find every thing I want à pointe nommée where ever I dip for it. This discovery indeed is almost of that kind which I call Serendipity, a very expressive word, which as I have nothing better to tell you, I shall endeavour to explain to you: you will understand it better by the derivation than by the definition. I once read a silly fairy tale, called the three Princes of Serendip: as their Highnesses travelled, they were always making discoveries, by accidents & sagacity, of things which they were not in quest of: for instance, one of them discovered that a mule blind of the right eye had travelled the same road lately, because the grass was eaten only on the left side, where it was worse than on the right—now do you understand Serendipity? one of the most remarkable instances of this accidental sagacity (for you must observe that no discovery of a thing you are looking for, comes under this description) was of my lord Shaftsbury, who happening to dine at Lord Chancellor Claren=don's, found out the marriage of the Duke of York & Mrs Hyde, by the res=pect with which her Mother treated her at table. I will send you the inscription in my next letter; you see I endeavour to grace your present as it deserves.

CAEPLLO

Volume 21, page 120. Walpole wrote Mann, 4 August 1757: 'I send you two copies . . . of a very honourable opening of my press—two amazing odes of Mr Gray—they are Greek, they are Pindaric, they are sublime—consequently I fear a little obscure.'

The copy shown is not one of Mann's, but, as Walpole wrote on it, 'The first book compleated at Strawberry Hill Aug. 4 1757.' He pasted it into a scrap book (Hazen 2506) for which he printed a label on the spine and a title-page, 'A Collection of all the Loose Pieces Printed at Strawberry Hill.'

O D E S

B Y

Mr. G R A Y.

[Price One Shilling.]

26. Sir Robert Walpole's Birth-Date

Volume 22, page 25. Walpole to Mann, 13 April 1762: 'Robert Walpole was born at Houghton in Norfolk, August 26th, 1675.'

Walpole (who was not at his best with dates and figures) persisted in saying his father was born in 1675. Collins's eighteenth-century peerage gives 1674, but the question is settled by Mary Burwell Walpole, Sir Robert's mother, in her Receipt Book, which is open here at 'ye age of all my children' and shows that her fifth and eldest surviving son, Robert, was born 'twenty six of August 1676.'

yͤ age of all my Chilldren

1 Susan was borne one wedenday yͤ 6 of June 1672

2 mary was borne one Sunday yͤ 8 eight of June 1673

3 Edward was borne on tuesday yͤ twenty third of June 1674

4 Burwell was borne on thursday yͤ twenty six of August 1675

5ᵗ Robert was borne on Saterday yͤ twenty six of August 1676

6 John was borne on munday yͤ third of September 1677

7 Horatio was born on Sunday yͤ eight december 1678

8 Christopher was born on fryday ye twenty of february 1679

9 elizabeth was born on thursday yͤ twenty fowrth march 1680

10 elizabeth was born on thursday yͤ seauenteenth october 1682

11 galfridus was born Saterday yͤ fifteenth march 1683

12 Ann was born munday yͤ six of Aprell 1685

13 dorathy was born Saterday yͤ eighteenth September 1686

14 Susan was born munday yͤ fift of december 1687

15 mordaunt was born thursday ye thirteenth december 1688

16 a boy still born yͤ eight of Aprell 1690

17 Charles was born ye thirty of June 1691

18 william was born fryday yͤ seauen of Aprell 1693

19 a daughter still born yͤ twenty of January 1694

yͤ age of my Daugh Hawcridg Chilldren

Richard was borne ones sunday yͤ first of August 1708

Susan was borne of thusday yͤ fowrthteenth of June 1709

lucy miscaryed of a boy nomber yͤ 26 1710

she miscaryed of a garle nomber yͤ 7 1711

Volume 23, page 556. This is the tract Walpole refers to in his letter to
Mann of 23 February 1774: 'There is just published a very good dialogue
between three persons of some note, namely, the partitioners of Poland.'
It is bound in volume 31 of his 'Tracts of the Reign of King George the
3d' (Hazen 1609:31.) Walpole began this collection on the King's acces-
sion to the throne in 1760 and kept it up for thirty-five years. He also made
collections of the 'Theatre of the reign of George the 3d' and 'Poems of
George the 3d.' Each volume has his arms on the sides and a 'List of Pieces
in this Volume' written by him on the inside covers; frequently, as here,
he has added a note on the author and the month when the piece appeared. The tracts and four-fifths of the plays are at Farmington, the
poems at Harvard. These collections formed part of Walpole's plan to
transmit to us the history of his time.

THE
POLISH·PARTITION,

ILLUSTRATED;

IN

SEVEN DRAMATICK DIALOGUES,

OR,

CONVERSATION PIECES,

BETWEEN

REMARKABLE PERSONAGES,

PUBLISHED FROM THE

MOUTHS AND ACTIONS

OF THE

INTERLOCUTORS.

BY GOTLIEB PANSMOUZER,
THE BARON'S NEPHEW.

by the Tutor of Prince Poniatowski at Cambridge.

Cantabit vacuus coram latrone viator.   JUVEN.
Trojanas ut opes et lamentabile regnum
Eruerint Danai.   VIRGIL.

LONDON:

PRINTED FOR P. ELMSLY, OPPOSITE SOUTHAMPTON-
STREET, IN THE STRAND.

February 1774.

28. 'View of Richmond-hill, Twickenham, and Mr Pope's house from the terrace at Strawberry-hill by Mr Pars 1772'

Volume 24, pages 134–35. In his letter of 23 October 1775, Walpole introduces William Pars to Mann as a young painter who 'has already great merit, and has done several things for me, particularly, washed drawings of Strawberry, of which he can talk to you very perfectly.' Walpole had this drawing and two others by Pars engraved for his *Description of Strawberry Hill*, 1784. Of the many 'painters of views' that he employed, Pars seems to have been his favourite.

The caption, 'View of Richmond-hill . . . ,' was written by Walpole on the back of the drawing.

Volume 25, page 400. Walpole to Mann, 30 April 1783: 'Our nabobs do not plunder the Indies under the banners of piety like the old Spaniards and Portuguese. I call Man *an aurivorous animal.*'

From its place in the notebook, this observation was recorded in April 1783. Walpole liked it so much that he preserved it in his *Works* ('Detached Thoughts,' iv. 368.)

Presumably, he had many pocket notebooks, but this is the only one that has come to light (Hazen 2616).

Letter to the E. of Shelb.re from a noble Earl (Lord Bellamont)
of the kingd. of Irel. upon the subj. of final explanation respecting
the legislative rights of Irel. Lond. jan.ry 1783.

D. Cornwallis's answ. to Sr Hen. Clinton on conduct of the
former during Campaign of 1781 in N. America. feb. 1783.

Man is an carnivorous animal

30. Conversation Piece by Thomas Patch

of Lord Beauchamp and His Friends, 1765

Volume 26, page 45. 'Patch was excellent in caricatura, and was in much favour with the young English nobility who visited Florence; many of whom allowed him to represent them and their governors ludicrously. Lord Beauchamp, son of the Earl of Hertford, has a large picture in oil done by Patch at Florence, full of these characters, of Lord Beauchamp, Earl Berkeley, Sir Watkin Williams Wynne and others.' A key to most of the characters is on the lower right of the canvas, which is 45 x 68 inches. Horace Mann is the second figure from the right, Beauchamp the fifth from the left. Walpole's correspondence with him, his first cousin once-removed, is in Volumes 38 and 39.

Volume 27 and half of Volume 26 contain the index to the Mann correspondence which has over 100,000 entries.

The index is open at the reference to Mann's portrait by John Astley, which is oil on canvas, 19 x 14½ inches. Walpole reported to Mann, 23 March 1752 OS, that the picture had arrived and that Conway, just back from Italy, said it was 'extremely like you: Mr Chute cannot bear it, says it wants your countenance and goodness, that it looks bonny and Irish. I am between both and should know it . . .'

32. Two of Lady Diana Beauclerk's Drawings

for Walpole's *The Mysterious Mother*, 1776

Volume 28, page 244. Walpole to Mason, 18 February 1776: 'Do I know nothing superior to Mr Gibbon? . . . I talk of great original genius. Lady Di Beauclerc has made seven large drawings in soot-water (her first attempt of the kind) for scenes of my *Mysterious Mother*. Oh! such drawings! Guido's grace, Albano's children, Poussin's expression, Salvator's boldness in landscape and Andrea Sacchi's simplicity of composition might perhaps have equalled them had they wrought all together very fine. . . .' Walpole's partiality to the talents of his friends is one of his more endearing qualities.

'The Beauclerc Closet,' he noted in a copy of his *Description of Strawberry Hill,* 1774 (Hazen 2523), 'was built on purpose to receive seven incomparable drawings of Lady Diana Beauclerc for Mr Walpole's tragedy of *The Mysterious Mother*. The beauty and grace of the figures and of the children are inimitable; the expression of the passions most masterly, particularly in the . . . resolution of the countess in the last scene; in which is a new stroke of double passion in Edmund, whose right hand is clenched and ready to strike with anger, the left hand relents. In the scene of the children, some are evidently vulgar, the others children of rank; and the first child, that pretends to look down and does leer upwards, is charming. . . . These sublime drawings, the first histories she ever attempted, were all conceived and executed in a fortnight.'

Volume 29, pages 368–69, an appendix to Walpole's letter of 9 January 1773 to Mason in which he says, 'Mr Garrick has cut out the scene of the grave-diggers in *Hamlet*. I hope he will be rewarded with a place in the French Academy.' Shown here is Walpole's 'Book of Materials, 1771,' open to a long note on 'Garrick's Alterations of Hamlet' that begins, 'In 1773 Mr Garrick produced his *Hamlet* altered, in which he had omitted the scene of the grave-diggers, from injudicious complaisance to French critics, and their cold regularity, which cramps genius.'

34. The Draft of Walpole's Last Codicil
to His Will

Volume 30, page 372. The draft was drawn 27 December 1796, and signed by Walpole's lawyer, Hall of the Poultry, with a note, 'To be transcribed on the parchment for that purpose and sent Home this Evening.'
  Walpole died ten weeks later.

I Horatio Earl of Orford having already made my last Will

and Testament bearing date the 18th day of May 1793 with a Codicil thereto bearing

date the 5th day of June 1793 do make this to be a further Codicil to my sd. Will

I give and devise unto my dear Sister Lady Maria Churchill Wife of Charles

Churchill Esqr. (over and above the Legacy given to or for her Use & Benefit in and

by my sd. Will) The Annual Rent Charge or Yearly sum of £200 of lawful

Money of Great Britain during the Term of her natural Life to be issuing out of

charged & chargeable upon All and every my Freehold Manors Messes Farms

Lands Tenemts. Mill Heredits & premes in my sd. Will ment. to be situate

lying & being in the County of Norfolk which descended to me as Heir at

Law of my Nephew George late Earl of Orford deced and not out of my Leaseh.

or personal Estates or any or either of them or any part thereof free and clean

of all Parliamentary & other Taxes Rates Charges Assessments and Deductions

whatsr. by two equal half Yearly Payments on Midsr. Day & Xtmas Day in every

year during the Life of my sd. Sister & the first payment thereof to begin & be made

on such of the said Days of Payment as shall first & next happen after my

decease And I do also give and grant unto my said Sister such & the like

powers & remedies for recovering & receiving the sd. Annual Rent charge or Yearly

sum of £200 by Distress Entry & perception of the Rents & profits of the said

Heredits & premes charged therewith or of a sufficient part thereof as are usual

& customary in Cases of Grants of Rent Charges payable out of Lands And it

is my Will & Meaning that the Anny or Yearly sum of £25 which I have

in and by my said Will given unto my Servant Philip Colomb during his life

①

35. Allan Ramsay's Portrait of Walpole, 1758

Volume 31, page 9. Oil on canvas. 24 x 19¾ inches. Walpole wrote, 17 October 1758, to Lady Hervey, an older friend to whom he dedicated his *Anecdotes of Painting:* 'Your Ladyship, I hope, will not think that such a strange thing as my own picture seems of consequence enough to me to write a letter about it: but obeying your commands does seem so; and lest you should return and think I had neglected it, I must say that I have come to town three several times on purpose, but Mr Ramsay (I will forgive him) has been constantly out of town—so much for that.'

Although two copies by Gogain of the portrait were known, the original disappeared until 1953 when it was found in a Scottish family that had probably inherited it from Mrs Damer.

Volume 32, page 304. Walpole to Lady Ossory, 13 July 1776: 'I am obey-ing the Gospel, and putting my house in order, am ranging my prints and papers, am *composing* books, in the literal sense, and in the only sense I will compose books any more, I am pasting Henry Bunbury's prints into a volume.' He also made up a second volume of them.

Henry William Bunbury (1750–1811), was one of the gentlemen artists that Walpole admired extravagantly, calling him 'the second Hogarth' in the final volume of his *Anecdotes of Painting*. The title-pages for the two Bunbury volumes were printed at the Strawberry Hill Press and are ap-parently unique. There are 187 prints and drawings in the collection (Hazen 3563).

ETCHINGS

BY

Henry William Bunbury, Efq;

AND

AFTER HIS DESIGNS.

Volume 33, page 518. Writing to Lady Ossory, 5 July 1786, Walpole fears that his bumper harvest of hay will not be sufficient to indemnify him for his purchase at the sale. His copy of the catalogue is open to his note on the Missal illuminated by Julio Clovio: 'Bought by Mr Horace Walpole—Mr Udney assured Mr W. he had seen six more by the same hand, but none of them so fine, or so well preserved, £169-1-0.' The Missal (Hazen 3786) is now in the John Carter Brown Library, Providence, R.I.

In the front of the catalogue Walpole pasted a signed note of four pages on the Duchess which is printed in *The Duchess of Portland's Museum*, with an Introduction by W. S. Lewis, The Grolier Club, 1936. He delighted in annotating catalogues of exhibitions as well as of auctions, mindful of the importance of provenance.

2944 A Lady's portrait, in a black drefs, with the hair in curls over the forehead, and large fingle drop ear-rings the initials of painter's name, *I-L*   4-0-0.

2945 A Gentleman's portrait, drefsed in black and gold armour, with a blue fafh, by *Peter Oliver*, very fine   10-0-0.

I do not beleive it Milton.

2946 Two miniatures of MILTON and his MOTHER, in the drefs of the times; undoubted originals, admirably painted, in a tortoife-fhell cafe   34-2-6.

2947 A *remarkable fine* MINIATURE HEAD of OUR SAVIOUR, by *Ifaac Oliver*, fet in gold. Nothing can exceed the gracefulnefs, benevolence, and meeknefs, exprefsed in this picture   21-0-0.

N. B. *It was purchafed out of the well-known Collection of the late* Dr. Mead.

2948 A very high finifhed portrait of a Gentleman, in a black drefs, by *Holbien* — 10-7-6.

2949 It's Companion, — — — by *Ditto* — 23-2-0.

MISSALS, &c.

bought by the Marquis of Carmarthen. The Duchefs of Portland gave 21 guineas for it at the Sale of James West Efq

2950 QUEEN ELIZABETH'S PRAYER BOOK, which contains Six Prayers, compofed by her Majefty, and written by her own hand (in the true spirit of devotion) in the neateft and moft beautiful manner upon VELLUM. Two of the Prayers are in the English language, one in Latin, one in Greek, one in Italian, and one in French; on the infide of the covers are the pictures of the DUKE D'ALANCON and the QUEEN, by *Hilliard:* the binding, black fhagreen, with enamelled clafps, and in the center of each is a ruby   106-1-0.

It was bought by Edward the bookfeller. The King had intended to buy it & give it to Eton College as having belonged to their founder, & had given an unlimited commifsion for it, but his commifsioner thought it too dear and let it go, & Edward would not sell it again.

2951 A *very fine* ILLUMINATED MISSAL, which was *prefented* by the DUTCHESS of BEDFORD, (Sifter to the Duke of Burgundy, and wife of John Duke of Bedford, Regent of France) to KING HENRY the Sixth, in the year 1430; upon the back of the leaf, (on which are the *original portaits* of the DUKE and ANN his Wife, DUTCHESS of BURGUNDY) is her Deed of Gift to the King. The fize of the book is 11 inches long, 7¼ wide, and 2¼ thick, bound in crimfon velvet, with GOLD CLASPS, on which are engraved the Harley, Cavendifh, and Holles arms, quartered   213-3-0.

bought by Mr Horace Walpole. Mr Udny afsured Mr W. he had seen six more by the same hand, but none of them so fine or so well preserved.

2952 A *moft beautiful* MISSAL, ILLUMINATED in a fuperior degree of ELEGANCE by the famous DON JULIO CLOVIO, which in richnefs and harmony of colouring, as well as the tafte and judgment of the defigns and ornaments, is, perhaps, fuperior to any thing of the kind. The book is in THE HIGHEST STATE OF PRESERVATION, and the COLOURS retain their ORIGINAL BRILLIANCY. It is inferibed to the moft noble DUKE D'ALANCON, by *Don Julio Clovio*, Anno 1537, and from him came into the pofsefsion of the EARL of ARUNDEL and SURREY, from whofe collection it was purchafed by EDWARD LORD HARLEY, EARL of OXFORD and MORTIMER. The fize 5 inches ¾ long, 4 inches wide, and 2½ thick, bound in black leather, ornamented with GOLD PLATES, COVERS, and CLASPS   169-1-0. *Anfou*

2953 The heads of the Twelve Cæfars, in alabafter . . . . 5-2-6.

END *of the* TWENTY-SEVENTH DAY's SALE.

TWENTY-

38. General Fitzwilliam's Tribute to Walpole

Volume 34, page 59, note 11. The Hon. John Fitzwilliam (1714–89), army officer, was a Richmond neighbour of Walpole's. The tribute is bound into his copy of the *Essay on Modern Gardening:* 'Richmond, Surrey, October 1785: General Fitzwilliam has often thought himself obliged to Mr Horace Walpole, who has not only given to him this book of his *Essay on Modern Gardening,* but also most of his other publications, a collection not only instructive, but very curious and entertaining.

'Mr Walpole is so well known and celebrated in the learned world, that it would be needless to speak of his works; but what would that part of it say of him, who, like me, have been honoured by his good will and attention? His natural talents, his cheerfulness, the sallies of his imagination, the liveliness of his manner, the unexpected impressions on the ear of those who hear and listen to him, comes on, like a shooting star, or like Uriel, gliding on a sunbeam [cf. *Paradise Lost*]. I never met him but with pleasure and never left him, but with regret.'

Richmond Surry October 1785.

Genral Fitzwilliam has often thought himself
obliged to Mr. Horace Walpole, Who, has not only given
to him this Book of his Essay on Modern Gardening
but also, most of his Other Publications; a Collection not
only Instructive, But, Very Curious and Entertaining.

    Mr. Walpole is So Well Known & Celebrated, in the
Learned World, that it Would be needless to Speak of his
Works; But, what would that Part of it, Say of him,
who, Like me, have been honored by his good Will and
attention?   His Natural Talents, his Chearfullness,
the Sallies of his Imagination, the Liveliness of his
Manner, the unexpected Impression on the Ear, of those
who hear and Listen to him, Comes on, like a Shooting
Star, Or, Like Uriel, gliding on a Sun Beam. I Never
Met him, but with Pleasure, and never Left him, but
with Regret.

39. Bentley's Designs for the Library at Strawberry Hill
40. Chute's Designs for the Library at Strawberry Hill

Volume 35, page 157. Walpole wrote Bentley, 19 December 1753: 'For the library, it [your design] cannot have the Strawberry imprimatur: the double arches and double pinnacles are most ungraceful; and the doors below the book-cases in Mr Chute's design have a conventual look, which yours totally wants.'

Bentley's drawings for Strawberry Hill were pasted by Walpole into this book with a title-page (the only one known) printed at the Press about 1760: 'Drawings and Designs by Richard Bentley, only Son of Dr. Bentley, Master of Trinity College Cambridge' (Hazen 3585). It is, I think, the most important book in Walpole's library. Of the 75 drawings in it, about half are of Strawberry Hill; among the rest are sketches for Gray's odes. Walpole wrote a manuscript title for Chute's drawings (Hazen 3490), 'Slight Sketches of Architecture by John Chute, Esq; of the Vine in Hampshire.' His note on the drawing shown is, 'One side of the library at Strawberry Hill, taken from a doorcase in Dugdale's Old St Paul's by Mr Chute.' These drawings by Walpole's colleagues on 'The Committee' that designed Strawberry Hill illustrate how they adapted Gothic details from the plates in such works as Dugdale's *St Paul's* and Dart's *Canterbury*. See also No. 53.

The Gothic Revival in architecture owes much to Bentley's and Chute's drawings.

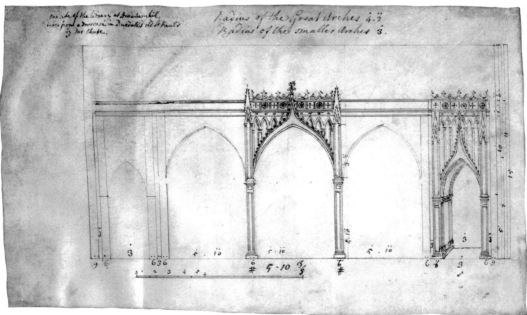

one side of the Library at Strawberryhill,
taken from a Doorcase in Dugdale's old St Paul's
for the Chapel.

Radius of the Great Arches 4.2
Radius of the smaller Arches 3.

Volume 36, page 19. Walpole to Sir Edward Walpole, ca 16 May 1745 OS: 'And for your love to your father, I have always declared, that of all his children I was convinced you loved him the best.'

Edward Walpole's sketches of his father are pasted into one of Horace Walpole's copies of his *Description of Strawberry Hill,* 1774 (Hazen 2523). On the cover to the lower one he noted, 'portrait of Sr Robert Walpole drawn by Sr Edward Walpole his second son.'

Before and After Its Alteration

Volume 37. Walpole wrote Conway, 8 June 1747: 'Twickenham. You perceive by my date that I am got into a new camp, and have left my tub at Windsor. It is a little play-thing-house that I got out of Mrs Chenevix's shop, and is the prettiest bauble you ever saw. It is set in enamelled meadows, with filigree hedges:

> A small Euphrates through the piece is roll'd,
> And little finches wave their wings in gold.

Two delightful roads, that you would call dusty, supply me continually with coaches and chaises: barges as solemn as Barons of the Exchequer move under my window; Richmond Hill and Ham Walks bound my prospect; but, thank God! the Thames is between me and the Duchess of Queensberry. Dowagers as plenty as flounders inhabit all around, and Pope's ghost is just now skimming under my window by a most poetical moonlight. I have about land enough to keep such a farm as Noah's, when he set up in the ark with a pair of each kind; but my cottage is rather cleaner than I believe his was after they had been cooped up together forty days.'

These sketches by Walpole are pasted into his copy of the *Description of Strawberry Hill,* 1774 (Hazen 2523).

Front of Sharberry Hill or the parson, as it was in 1747, before it was altered.

130

43. Miss Berry as Editor

Volume 38. Walpole to Lady Ailesbury, 20 July 1761. Miss Berry deleted the passages she put in square brackets when she printed this letter in Walpole's *Works*. Some of her deletions were inspired by prudery, some were made to spare the sensibilities of living persons, some to remove passages she considered dull. She pasted five footnotes on the first page. Her style of editing continued to the present century.

Volume 39. Walpole to Lady Ailesbury, 15 January 1775: 'You must know, Madam, that near Bath is erected a new Parnassus, composed of three laurels, a myrtle tree, a weeping-willow, and a view of the Avon, which has been new christened Helicon. . . . They [the Millers] hold a Parnassus-fair every Thursday, give out rhymes and themes, and all the flux of quality at Bath contend for the prizes. A Roman vase dressed with pink ribbands and myrtles receives the poetry, which is drawn out every festival; six judges of these Olympic games retire and select the brightest compositions, which the respective successful acknowledge, kneel to Mrs Calliope [Miller], kiss her fair hand, and are crowned by it with myrtle, with—I don't know what.'

In his copy of the *Poetical Amusements* (Hazen 2420), Walpole wrote an extensive note on the Millers that concludes: 'They instituted their poetical games, gave out subjects, Mrs Miller distributed prizes, and became perfectly ridiculous. Many persons of distinction humoured them and shared in their follies, while others laughed. Mr Anstey author of the inimitable Bath Guide, which even he himself could never imitate, exposed himself egregiously by becoming their champion and by writing with passion and stupidity against a clergyman who had satirized them in the newspapers. . . .

HW.'

Walpole kept the book locked up in the Glass Closet in his library away from the eyes of visitors.

W. Hibbart Bath.

POETICAL
AMUSEMENTS
AT A
VILLA
NEAR
BATH.

PRINTED BY R. CRUTTWELL,
For L. BULL, Bookfeller, in BATH:
And fold, in LONDON, by
HAWES, CLARKE, and COLLINS, in Pater-nofter-Row.
M DCC LXXV.

45. Grosvenor Bedford's Copy of Walpole's

Aedes Walpolianae, 1747

Volume 40. Grosvenor Bedford was Walpole's deputy at the Exchequer from 1755 to his death in 1771; his mother's family was close to the Walpoles. He wrote his name on a fly-leaf of this copy and 'the Gift of the Honble Horace Walpole.' Walpole in 'Short Notes' of his life pointed out that the *Aedes* was 'very incorrectly printed.' He corrected the 200 copies himself, beginning with the '44' under Sir Robert's portrait in the frontispiece.

ÆDES WALPOLIANÆ:

OR, A

DESCRIPTION

OF THE

Collection of Pictures

AT

Houghton-Hall in Norfolk,

The SEAT of the Right Honourable

Sir ROBERT WALPOLE,

EARL of ORFORD.

Artists and Plans reliev'd my solemn Hours;
I founded Palaces, and planted Bow'rs.
PRIOR's *Solomon.*

LONDON: Printed in the Year 1747.

46.   Col. Charles and Lady Mary Churchill

and Their Eldest Son by J. G. Eccardt, ca 1750

Volume 41. Oil on canvas, 9½ x 7¼ inches. Churchill was the natural son of General Charles Churchill, the first Duke of Marlborough's brother; Lady Mary was Sir Robert Walpole's natural daughter. This picture was 'taken,' Walpole tells us in the *Description of Strawberry Hill,* 'from the picture at Blenheim, of Rubens, his wife and child,' and so marked Churchill's connection with the seat of his father's family. Walpole hung the picture in the Blue Bedchamber at Strawberry with portraits, all by Eccardt, of Conway, Lady Ailesbury, and their daughter (afterwards Mrs Damer), Sir Charles Hanbury Williams, Thomas Gray, Richard Bentley, and Walpole himself.

47. The Duc de Nivernais's Translation of

Walpole's *Modern Gardening,* 1785

Volume 42. Walpole wrote the Duc de Nivernais, the French Ambassador to England, 1 February 1785: 'The interval however, allows me to ask a great favour, in order that I may produce an edition as little unworthy of the work as shall be in my power. The copy I had the honour of receiving is written in such very small characters, that my printer, unaccustomed to French manuscript, would make endless mistakes and confusion. Might I take the liberty of begging that the Duc de Nivernais would order one of his secretaries to send me another copy transcribed in a very large and distinct hand of both the text and notes, with stops and accents exactly as he would please to have the whole printed? I could not even trust my own diligence and attention without this assistance.'

The manuscript is Hazen 2617. Walpole wrote on the inside cover, 'This beautiful manuscript was written at Paris in 1785 by order of the Duc de Nivernais, Mr Walpole having desired to have a very accurate and legible copy of the Duke's translation, that the printer at Strawberry Hill, who was not accustomed to print French, nor indeed understood it, might make no mistakes. From this MS the edition was printed.

Hor. Walpole.'

ON MODERN GARDENING

BY Mr. HORACE WALPOLE.

*G*ARDENING *was probably one of the first arts that succeeded to that of building houses, and naturally attended property and individual possession. Culinary, and afterwards medicinal herbs, were the objects of every head of a family: it became convenient to have them within reach, without seeking them at random in woods, in meadows, and on mountains, as often as they were wanted. When the earth ceased to furnish spontaneously all these primitive luxuries, and culture became requisite, separate inclosures for rearing herbs grew expedient. Fruits were in the same predicament, and those most in use or that demand attention, must have entered into and extended the domestic inclosure. The good man Noah, we are told, planted a vineyard, drank of the wine, and was drunker, and every body knows the consequences. Thus we acquired kitchen-gardens*

ESSAI SUR L'ART DES JARDINS MODERNES,

PAR M. HORACE WALPOLE,

Traduit en François par M. LE DUC DE NIVERNOIS, en 1784.

L'ART DES JARDINS a succédé vraisemblablement un des premiers à celui de la Bâtisse, & il a dû naturellement suivre la propriété & la possession individuelle. Les herbes de Cuisine & ensuite les plantes médicinales étoient l'objet des soins de chaque Chef de Famille: il convint de les avoir à portée sans les chercher au hazard dans les Bois, dans les Prairies, sur les Montagnes chaque fois qu'on en avoit besoin. Quand la terre cessa de fournir spontanément toutes ces premières commodités & qu'elle eût besoin de culture, il parut à propos d'avoir des Enclos séparés pour élever des Plantes. Les fruits étoient en même considération & ceux qui sont le plus d'usage ou qui demandent le plus d'attention durent entrer dans ces enclos domestiques & en augmenter l'étendue. Le bon homme Noé, dit-on, planta la vigne, bût du vin & s'enyvra; & chacun sçait les conséquences. Nous eûmes donc des Pota-

gers.

48. One of Bertie Greatheed's Drawings in Walpole's Copy of the Bodoni *Castle of Otranto*, 1791

Volume 43. Walpole wrote the elder Greatheed, 22 February 1796: 'I am so delighted and think myself so much honoured by having contributed to inspire young Mr Greatheed with such speaking conceptions, that you cannot be surprised, if after meditating for above two days on the pleasure they gave me, I cannot sit down contented with a transient view, and with the bare recollection of every circumstance and attitude that struck me—and yet could I design at all like your son, I am certain that I could sketch out at least the disposition of every one of the four drawings, and of every one of the principal characters . . . Will it then be taking too great a liberty, Sir, to own how much you would add to the great obligation you have already conferred on me, to allow me to have copies made of these astonishing drawings—you can depend on the care my own vanity would make me take of the originals, which my gratitude would oblige me to restore as safely.'

Walpole bound the four drawings, whether the originals or the copies is not clear, in this copy of the Bodoni *Otranto* (Hazen 3729). The drawing illustrates the end of the novel when 'the walls of the castle . . . were thrown down with a mighty force, and the form of Alfonso, dilated to an immense magnitude, appeared in the centre of the ruins.'

49. The Manuscript of the Journal of the

Printing Office

A Bibliography of the Strawberry Hill Press, by Allen T. Hazen, Yale University Press, 1942; and the reissue by Dawsons of Pall Mall, London, 1973.

Walpole kept this Journal from the Press's opening in 1757 to its close with the printing of Hannah More's 'Bishop Bonner's Ghost' in 1789. It is a complete record of the books printed at the Press, but lacks several of the 'Detached Pieces.' It is 2506 in Hazen.

Journal of the Printing-Office at Strawberry hill
near Twickenham in Middlesex.

1757.
June 25ᵗʰ. The Press was erected. Wᵐ Robinson, printer.
July 16ᵗʰ Began to print. The first work was an edition of two new
Odes by Mr Gray: one, on the power & progress of Poetry;
the other, on the destruction of the Welsh Bards by Edward 1ˢᵗ
Aug. 3ᵈ 1000 copies of the Odes finished.
＿ 8ᵗʰ 2000 copies published by Dodsley. ——
... began to print Hentznerus's account of England, with a
translation by Rich. Bentley; the advertisement by H. Walpole.
18ᵗʰ Mr müntz printed for his first essay a sonnet written that
evening by Mr Walpole on killing Time; the thought from
a French epigram. * (see on tother side)
19ᵗʰ Lucy Younge, Countess of Rochford, Etheldeda Viscountess Townshend
Miss Bland, & James Earl Waldegrave dining at Strawberryhill,
were carried to see the printing-office, where the following lines
being ready prepared were taken off;
                For Lady Townshend;
            The Press speaks:.
From Me Wits and Poets their glory obtain;
Without Me their Wit & their Verses were vain:
Stop, Townshend! and let me but Print what You say;
You, the fame I on others bestow, will repay.

        Lady Rochford desiring to see the manner of composing
for the press, four lines from a play were given to the

In the reissue of the *Bibliography* Dr Hazen has recorded new copies and new locations. One of the few amendments is *A Collection of Prints, Engraved by Various Persons of Quality,* which turned up after the *Bibliography* was published. It has four title-pages printed at the Press. Walpole described the book to Mason, 7 May 1775: 'I have invented a new and very harmless way of *making books.* . . . I have just made a *new book.* . . . It is a volume of etchings by *noble authors*. They are bound in robes of crimson and gold: the titles are printed at my own press, and the pasting is *by my own hand.'*

A Bibliography of Horace Walpole, by Allen T. Hazen, page 177. The unpublished manuscript of Walpole's 'Memoirs of the Reign of King George III, 1783–1791.' Walpole's *Last Ten Years of the Reign of King George II,* his *Memoirs of the Reign of King George III, 1760–1771,* and his *Last Journals, 1771–1783,* were mutilated by their nineteenth-century editors who 'improved' the text by cutting and altering it. The Yale Edition of Horace Walpole's *Memoirs* will be edited by Mr John Brooke and we shall then have at long last what Walpole wrote, fully annotated.

In September the stocks fell to 59, tho' Peace made even with Holland.

Violent resolutions of the Volunteers at Dungannon in Ireland, particularly for shortening of Parliaments. Extravagant speech of Lord Bristol Bp of Derry for that purpose. The Duke of Richmond had wrote to them a favourable answer to their Letter.

Ld Geo. Gordon made some objections to the Resolutions sent to him from Edinburgh; & said Parson Wyvill & the English associations had made themselves ridiculous.

Lord George was called upon in print to produce his accusations ag.t the English Ministers, to which he made no reply. He accused himself of having bought Luggershall.

A seat for Winchester being vacated, the Duke of Chandos recommended Mr Blood, the Duke's Secretary to it.

Lord Shelburne, D Thurlow & W. Pitt at Paris.

October.

The York Association revived. They renewed Resolutions for reform of Parliament, & censured the Coalition with Lord North, as the Minister of the American War, tho' without naming him.

Mr Wyvill had written to the Irish Volunteers, to encourage them in reforming Parliament, & they printed his letter.

What contradictions in these Demagogues! Ld Bristol had vehemently urged Ld North & his associates to more violence ag.t the Americans. Being neglected, he was now a Patriot. The Duke of Chandos had been a fulsome Courtier: turned Patriot on not obtaining the Government of the Isle of Wight. Being neglected by Lord Rockingham he was now in opposition again, & brought the Irish Mr Blood into Parl.t for Winchester.

Lord George Gordon fell on the Yorkshire Associators, tho' Mr Mason one of the Heads, was eager against Papists.

Mr Mason, tho' eager against Papists, leagues with the Irish Volunteers, tho' Lord Bristol was a zealous Advocate for Toleration of them; & France notoriously had dealings with them. The Committee, who seemed to want support from the County, by begging for it, thanked Mr Pitt for his behaviour the last year in his reform bill — yet some of the members had been sensible that he was not sincerely for it — he was then in place — now is out.

Violent letter, published in the papers, from D Hervey to Lord Howe, on the latter transmitting to the former the thanks of the House of Commons to him & the Officers for their behaviour at the siege of Gibraltar. At the same time was published another letter from D Hervey to D Howe begging his pardon for having unjustly accused him of want of courage & veracity. These seemed to come from D Howe, for very soon was printed a letter from D Hervey to the Printer of the newspaper, saying he was never ashamed of owning it when he had been in the wrong; that he was satisfied of D Howe's courage, but that from want of judgment he had ruined his country.

The story is, I heard it from good authority, was this. D Hervey & some other young Sea officers had remonstrated ag.t D Howe's discipline in America — he bore with them, without relenting. D Hervey took the opportunity of their disgrace of his letter, to find fault with D Howe, & the opportunity of his reading them the thanks of the H.t of Commons to write that opprobrious letter. As soon as D Hervey landed, D Howe sent Capt. Leveson to him demanding him to sign a recantation or to challenge him. They met with swords. D Hervey refused to sign; D Howe then insisted on fighting. D Hervey then said he would sign the letter if he might alter one word: D Howe consented, if it was just. D Howe asked if he had shown the letter! Yes, to one person. To no more? yes, he did not say he had — then I must too, s.d D Howe — if you had not, I should not have said any thing of it — yet after all this, did D Hervey write his letter to the Printer!

52. Bentley's Frontispiece to Walpole's

Last Ten Years of George II

Richard Bentley's frontispiece to Walpole's *Last Ten Years of the Reign of King George II,* a pen and ink drawing, $11\frac{3}{4}$ x $6\frac{3}{4}$ inches, inscribed by Walpole, 'R. Bentley f.' The author is portrayed sitting between Heraclitus and Democritus before the east front of Strawberry Hill, which was largely the work of Bentley.

FARI QUÆ SENTIAT

R. Bentley f.

53.   Walpole's Copy of Sandford's
Kings of England, 1677

Hazen, *A Catalogue of Horace Walpole's Library*, Volume I, No. 581.
The book (Hazen 581) is open to the plate of the screen of Prince Arthur's
tomb in Worcester Cathedral. The notes in pencil are by Walpole and,
probably, Richard Bentley and show how the Strawberry Committee chose
and adapted Gothic sepulchral monuments for the embellishment of Strawberry Hill. In his *Description* of it Walpole wrote that the hall was 'hung
with gothic paper, printed by one Tudor, from the screen of Prince
Arthur's tomb in the cathedral of Worcester' (*Works* ii. 401).

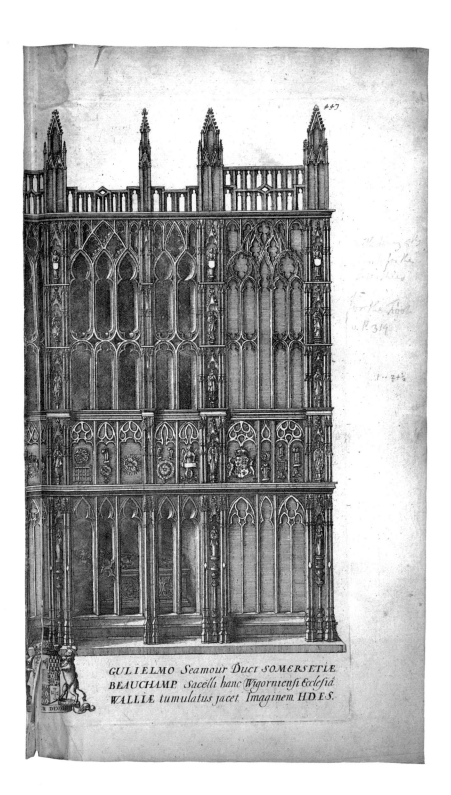

GULIELMO Seamour Duci SOMERSETIÆ.
BEAUCHAMP. Sacelli hanc Wigorniensi Ecclesiâ
WALLIÆ tumulatus jacet, Imaginem. H.D.F.S.

54.   Mason's Alterations to Walpole's

Mysterious Mother

Hazen, *A Catalogue of Horace Walpole's Library,* Volume II, No. 2528. Mason wrote his 'alterations' in this copy of the *Mysterious Mother,* Strawberry Hill, 1768, and in his letter to Walpole of 8 May 1769. Walpole thanked him promptly for his 'kindness,' in making his alterations, assuring him that 'I shall correct my own copy by them.' What he really thought of them he wrote at the bottom of Mason's letter:

'N.B. I did not adopt these alterations because they would totally have destroyed my object, which was to exhibit a character whose sincere penitence was not degraded by superstitious bigotry. The introduction of jealousy was utterly foreign to the subject . . .' Signed 'H. Walpole.'

THE

Myſterious Mother.

A

TRAGEDY.

By Mr. HORACE WALPOLE.

with mſſ alterations by Mr Mason.

Sit mihi ſas audita loqui!   VIRGIL.

PRINTED AT STRAWBERRY-HILL:
MDCCLXVIII.

55. Walpole's Postscript to His *Historic Doubts*
of Richard III, 1793

Hazen, *A Catalogue of Horace Walpole's Library,* Volume III, No. 3909. Walpole bound this manuscript into one of five known copies of his *Works,* 1770. 'It is afflictive,' he wrote, 'to have lived to find in an age called not only civilized but enlightened, in this eighteenth century, that such horrors, such unparalleled crimes have been displayed on the most conspicuous theatre in Europe, in Paris the rival of Athens and Rome, that I am forced to allow that a multiplicity of crimes, which I had weakly supposed were too manifold and too absurd to have been perpetrated even in a very dark age, and in a northern island not only not commencing to be polished, but enured to barbarous manners . . . I must *now* believe that any atrocity may have been attempted or practised by an ambitious Prince of the blood aiming at the crown in the fifteenth century . . .' Philip Duke of Orléans in plotting the death of his cousin Louis XVI was 'a monster about whose abominable actions one could not entertain one historic doubt.'

Postscript
to my Historic Doubts,
written in Febr. 1793.

It is afflictive to have lived to find in an Age called not only
civilized but enlightened, in this eighteenth Century, that such horror,
such unparalleled Crimes have been displayed on the most conspicuous
Theatre in Europe, in Paris the rival of Athens & Rome, that I am
forced to allow that a multiplicity of Crimes, which I had weakly supr
=posed were too manifold & too absurd to have been perpetrated even
in a very dark age, & in a northern Island not only not commencing
to be polished, but enured to barbarous manners, and hardened by
long & barbarous civil Wars amongst Princes & nobility strictly related, —
— yes, I must now believe that any atrocity may have been
attempted or practised by an ambitious Prince of the blood aiming
at the Crown in the fifteenth Century. I can believe [I do not say I do] that
Richard Duke of Gloucester dipped his hand in the blood of the
Saint-like Henry the 6th, tho so revolting & injudicious an act as to
excite the indignation of mankind against him. I can now believe
that he contrived the death of his own Brother Clarence — and I can
think it possible — inconceivable as it was — that he aspersed the
chastity of his own Mother, in order to bastardize the Offspring of
his Eldest Brother; for all these extravagant excesses have been
exhibited in the compass of five years by a Monster, by a Royal Duke,
who has actually surpassed all the guilt imputed to Richard the 3d;
and who, devoid of Richard's courage, has acted his enormities openly,